Fasting for Breakthrough

Fasting for Breakthrough

A Guide to Praying in Faith

Myles Holmes

ISBN: 1505247624
ISBN 13: 9781505247626

Table of Contents

Fasting Faq's

Why another book on fasting and prayer? Are there not hundreds if not thousands of books on the subject? Yes, and many of those are in my library and have been a great blessing to me. However, the need is so great and the hour so late. We are still lacking power and authority. There are prayers yet to be answered. There are dreams and visions still to unfold. If my writing can encourage a few more thousand believers to take up GOD's mandate to radically alter the world through prayer and fasting, then all of this will be worth my humble efforts. This is my seed into your life for miracles, signs and wonders and breakthroughs.

What is a "Breakthrough"? One definition is "a sudden, important development or success, a discovery, innovation or revolution."

A Breakthrough may also be defined as —

- Ability to see, know or do something you never could before
- Advancing through obstacles that were once insurmountable
- Becoming a conqueror over what once conquered you

We must have BREAKTHROUGHS! Our world is now saturated with crises. We seem to be quickly sliding toward the edge of total moral, social and economic collapse. Violence increases on our streets, international and domestic jihadist terror groups grow stronger by the day, our media and entertainment is becoming more vile and perverted by the hour, governments are amassing un-sustainable debt loads and there is no answer from anywhere.

Those who look to the Church for hope are often disappointed by the lack of authority and power they find under the steeple. When we should be the true harbors of Hope and Change, we have allowed political parties to steal our thunder, when they have no lightning!

The two most critical signs of a church that has exchanged the prophetic mantle for pathetic models is the lack of fire in the pulpit and the missing fervency in the Prayer Closet.

First, in order to obtain lasting spiritual breakthrough, a genuine church-wide and culture-shifting revival, there must be a return to the passionate, powerful preaching of the Full Gospel. We must do away with jelly-fish, no back-bone Christianity. We must do away with spineless Christianity.

Spineless Christianity

Spineless Christianity is created by preachers with no Bible Backbone!

- No preaching about Creation.
- No teaching about sexuality and morality.
- No preaching about the sins of homosexuality, abortion or pornography.
- No preaching against godless, blaspheming politicians.
- No teaching on the evil of the satanic religion of islam.
- No preaching about Hell and eternal judgment.
- No teaching on humility, brokenness and repentance.
- No preaching on the power of prayer and fasting.
- No teaching on the supremacy of Christ and Christian culture.
- No preaching on the return of Christ.
- No preaching that Jesus is the only WAY to the Father.

Preachers, ask GOD for the anointing of Elijah, John the Baptist and the Apostles. Most of them died for their ministry; today, too many are living for theirs! If we are in hot pursuit of the Last Days-Revival, it must start in the pulpit.

Spineless, sissified preachers must be great dancers, I am sure, because they can dance, spin, twirl, pirouhette and leap all around the Truth and never touch it!

I remember, all of the old preachers I grew up with, including my grampa and my dad, always had a bit of gravel in their voice, a bit of a rasp, no high-pitch, apologetic whine, but an authority mixed with a bit of gravel, not anger or hatefulness, not gruff or growling, but a passion that came from a deep place. I did not realize it then, but now I know that it was from years of hard preaching and decades of crying out to God in intercession. I am humbly grateful to report that at 53, there is now a bit of gravel in my voice.

So, join me in a prophetic declaration over our pulpits...

- No more pansies in the pulpit.
- No more sycophants in this struggle.
- No more wimps in this war.
- No more crybabies in this crisis.
- No more backsliders in this battle.
- No more chumps in this challenge.
- No more cowards in this conflict.
- Man up, pray up, look up, or ship out!

Ministry in today's confused world leaves only two stark choices - blatantly pathetic or Biblically prophetic. There is no middle road to take.

Secondly, and just as critical as the lack of fire in the pulpit, is the neglect of the authority that is only found on our knees, through prayer and fasting. Some strongholds require more than prayer; the intercession must be coupled with fasting to seek the Favor and Face of GOD.

If you want all GOD has in reserve for you in these last days, if you are desperate for bondages to be broken and strongholds to be demolished and victories realized in your personal life, family, church, city and nation, then join me on a spiritual adventure over the next 21 days.

GOD has never answered a prayer that has not been prayed. He *has* promised that if we His people, are humble, repentant, and will seek His Face, He will hear from Heaven, forgive our sins, and He will heal our land. That is something we cannot live without!

Make a genuine commitment, whether this is your first fast, or your 30th, that you will keep a daily appointment with GOD. This is not about rules, or religion or works or trying harder. It is about discipline.

Make this a serious fast that actually costs something. Giving up Krispy Kreme Donuts for 21 days is not a fast. Sacrifice, pay a price, lay down your rights and for these 21 days give GOD your best, then watch Him do the rest!

My 21 Day Commitment

"For these 21 days, so that I may give to GOD a season of fervent worship, intense intercession with increased time and attention given to prayer; so that I may discipline my body and bring it under subjection to GOD's Spirit within me, so that I may access more power from GOD; as His Spirit empowers me and by His Grace....I will be fasting (abstaining from)" _____

    I will be Fasting and Praying for BREAKTHROUGH in these areas in my life…

Spiritual Hunger _____
Family Salvation _____
Physical Needs, Healing _____
Financial Needs _____
My Home Church _____
The United States of America or your nation _____
Israel & the Peace of Jerusalem _____

    Remember a fast is much more than simply going WITHOUT something, it is going WITH Someone! Go with GOD! Fasting without prayer is no better than a fad diet. Get ALONE with GOD and talk some, but listen more. EXPECTATION!

"Whatever you do, do all to the Glory of GOD."

1 Cor. 10:31

Fasting Guidelines

I can personally testify that all of the most significant breakthroughs in my life have come during, or just after, a serious, extended season of fasting and prayer. My best ideas come during prayer times, but the financial miracles, supernatural direction, and Heavenly blessing that have marked my life have always been closely linked to prayer and fasting. There is a release of power, anointing and authority that is only available through prayer and fasting. Matthew 17:21. We are bringing our bodies into submission and seeking GOD intensely during these days.

Please carefully consider the following.

- If you are elderly, a young teenager, pregnant or nursing a baby, do not consider fasting at this time. You have neither my blessing nor permission to do so.
- If you are on any kind of medication please consult your doctor before considering any type of fast.
- It is very wise to consider taking as long to prepare for a fast and to come off of the fast, as the length of time you were on the fast. Doing this gently, is the key. No abrupt changes.
- Of course, seek the LORD's direction. Ask the LORD, when, and how long?

With these guidelines in place, let me give you a few ideas for a fast.

1. Daniel Fast - water, fruit and plain vegetables, this can be extended.
2. Mild Juices Fast - no acidic juices, for shorter periods.
3. Water Only Fast - one or two days only recommended, drink lots of water.
4. Fasting One Meal a day, or one day a week.
5. Fasting Sleep- for one night to seek GOD.
6. Complete TV Fast - Break the power of this box in your life.
7. Total Social Media Fast.
8. Total Internet Fast- other than work-related.

The premise behind a spiritual fast is not deprivation, but discipline and time allocation. The extra time you would be preparing and eating your meal is now available for an audience with the King.

- The hunger headaches will subside in two or three days.
- If you are abstaining from a caffeine habit, this will cause headaches for a couple of days as well.
- The throbbing hunger in your gut will subside in 4 to 5 days.

You will begin to notice a deeper sense of intimacy with Christ and the revelation of His Spirit.

Don't you dare look long- faced, depressed or deprived. (Matt. 6:16) Go back to your food or you will give fasting a bad name! This is Glory- time, this is Power- time; believe and you will receive!

Let's be honest, during this fast, we are seeking more power with GOD. We need more answers. We are desperately in need of more results. The harvest is yet to be reaped, and there are millions outside of God's grace. And we have tried all the best and brightest and biggest that the world has to offer. We have come to the conclusion that we must have more power with God.

Do You Want More Power With God?

The one vital secret to gaining more power, authority and anointing from and with GOD is so simple, and so contrary to our humanity, that it is routinely ignored, thus explaining the weakness of much of our experience, and the sad loss of spiritual potential. Here it is.

More power from GOD is always for others, not for yourself.

JESUS said, "The greatest among you is the servant." You can live your whole life and miss this simplicity.   Or, you can live for others and minister to others and serve others while walking in miracle-producing, power-anointing and signs & wonders ministry.

The choice is yours, the Glory is GOD's!

Remember, the genuine Pentecostal Power and Anointing of the Holy Spirit does not come to insult our minds or to make us look weird. He comes to make us more like JESUS!

Breaking Personal and Spiritual Strongholds

We will be praying and fasting toward these specific areas for 21 days.

1. Spiritual Life
2. Marriage- Present or Future
3. Children
4. Grandchildren -Born or Yet to Be
5. Finances
6. Physical Health
7. Mental and Emotional Life
8. Pride, Rebellion and Stubbornness
9. Prayerlessness
10. Fear
11. Anger
12. Resistance to Change
13. Inability to Keep My Mouth Shut
14. Tolerance of Sin In My Own Life
15. Addiction to Food
16. Lack of Passion for the Lost
17. Lack of Submission to Spiritual Authority
18. Our Nation
19. The World and Israel
20. Our Church
21. Releasing Revival and Harvest

Breakthrough in Your Spiritual Life

Our 21 day fast begins! Thank you for joining us on an intensive journey into the heart of GOD. We are going without food, or sleep or regular entertainment, to find more time to seek the Presence of the Holy Spirit and the Blessing of Heaven in our lives. We are doing this because we need CHANGE.

Everything about us resists the CHANGE we require but we push through. Since we are creatures of comfort, since we love the precision of a predictable pattern, we can very easily fall into the trap of tradition and the sin of sameness. We forget that growth requires CHANGE, that real growth requires real change and that massive growth requires massive change. We somehow forget that nothing on this planet produces fruit without CHANGE.

When we have determined at all costs to hang on to what was, we completely miss what could be. Fasting is one of the most certain ways of embracing Heaven's change in our spiritual life. Old things have passed away and all things have become new, but all things must _continue_ to pass away and all things must _continue_ to become new.

There is no room in the child of GOD's life for spiritual complacency, lethargy, sameness or satisfaction. Fasting helps us to refocus on spiritual hunger and appetite for Kingdom Revelation. As you seek GOD today in prayer and over the next 21 days, I dare you to pray this kind of prayer -

"Almighty GOD, my Loving Heavenly Father, please change me, change my heart, change my mind, change my personality, change my attitude, CHANGE me Lord, more and more to be less and less like me and more like Your Son Jesus!"

If you have no desire to pray that kind of prayer and have no realization that you actually need to change, if you do not WANT to change, then you are in deep and serious spiritual trouble. However, if you can say "LORD, I want to want to!", that's enough for GOD to work with!

If that *is* your prayer during this fast, than I can assure you that you have embarked on a rich season of transformation from glory to glory, from revelation to revelation and from WOW to WOW! Many of us are going without solid food, some are doing a Daniel Fast. But whatever personal discipline you are subjecting your body to, understand you DO need plenty of liquids! And you need plenty of the Word of GOD and prayer.

Fasting without time in GOD's Presence is simply a fad diet. Fasting in GOD's Presence releases miraculous power and spiritual revelation. This is to humble you, not to elevate you. If you sense pride or arrogance or a religious spirit arising, repent and rebuke it. I also strongly urge you to journal what the Spirit of GOD is speaking to you during these 21 days. It will be a wonderful record of the beautiful testimony of your experience in GOD's workshop!

Praying with you for your breakthrough.

Breaking Through Marriage Strongholds – Present or Future

Today we are seeking GOD for His presence and power and blessing in our marriages. If you are married at the moment, you need GOD's blessing. If you are not married, there is a distinct possibility you will be in the future, because you can be too young to be married, but you can never be too old to find someone sweet to share the rest of your life with.

I don't need to convince you that marriage is under attack today, not just the definition of what marriage is, not only the institution that defines society, but your particular marriage has no doubt found itself to be a major target of the enemy. Why is that? It is very simple, satan is extremely terrorized by pure love, exceptionally threatened by the power of unity and exceedingly intimidated by a husband and wife who understand that they are to live out their marriage as a direct image of Christ's relationship with the church!

That's why marriage is so much more than only a physical union or emotional bond. Marriage is a spiritual command center, a place where GOD intends to set up a little Heaven on earth, where His Kingdom can come and His Will be done. Now, we all fail, our expectations fall short, and the incredible heart-stopping, overwhelming affection of our wedding day can often be overcome by years of disappointment and disillusionment. That's why we must seek the blessing of GOD, the fullness of the Spirit and the Power of His Presence to fill our homes.

It certainly may look like a problem in the romance department or the finance department or some other segment of your busy and frustrated life, but I can assure you that problems in your marriage are actually spiritual problems that need a spiritual solution! There is no better time than this fast to seek GOD for His Grace to enable you to offer forgiveness to your spouse and put aside all bitterness, self-centeredness and anger.

This would be the time to begin to open the Word of GOD and pray with your spouse daily. Buy a devotional book for couples if you need to, but if you can't pray with your spouse you have just proven you have a spiritual problem. If you pray privately or with others but never with your spouse, begin to repent right now and ask your lover for forgiveness. The old cliché is nonetheless true, the family or marriage that prays together, stays together. We simply must stop taking each other for granted.

Your children and grandchildren need a solid witness of a loving marriage, and it is possible with GOD's help. If you want a better marriage, work for it, fight for it, faith for it and pray for it. The world is waiting to see what can be done through an army of loving husbands and wives who allow no strife to hinder the anointing, who walk in the power of the Word and are living examples to neighbors, friends and loved ones.

As you fast today, place your marriage on the altar and ask GOD to rain down His Fire upon your heart, then take your sweetheart's hands in yours and tell them they better get ready for a brand-new man or woman! LOVE on each other, the reward is more than worth the investment!

Praying and believing with you for your breakthrough.

Breaking Strongholds in Your Children

Stay strong in faith as you fast and pray today, especially for your children. We love our kids! They mean more than life to us and they have brought more joy to our hearts than we could ever have dreamed possible.

Yet these same children can break our hearts and cause us sleepless nights of tears, worries and concern. During this fast I encourage you to remember one simple fact about our children. They are GOD's children.

He knew about them and loved them before they were ever conceived. And He knows them better than we do.

We must stay in prayer and faith, constantly and continually decreeing the Word of GOD over our children.

- "My seed will be mighty on the earth!" Psalm 112:1
- "All my children shall be taught by the LORD and great will be the peace of my children." Isaiah 54:13
- "GOD's Word will not return to me void, it will accomplish its purpose it will prosper in my children's hearts." Isaiah 55:11
- "As for me and my house, we will serve the LORD." Joshua 24:15
- "God's glory will appear to my children." Psalm 90:16
- "My sons and daughters will prophesy." Acts 2:17
- "My children are coming back from the land of the enemy." Jer. 31:15
- "Blessed is the fruit of my womb." Deut. 28:4

- "I will contend with him who contends with you and I will save your children." Isaiah 49:25

You need to find the Word of GOD that applies to your particular home and decree it, declare it and prophesy it over your children daily. The Word says, "What you bind on earth will be bound in Heaven and what you loose on earth will be loosed in Heaven!" So, take up your mantle as a prophet and priest over your home! The battle for our children will only become more intense in the days ahead. But the weapons we fight with are not fleshly or human, they are mighty in GOD for pulling down strongholds.

Remember His Promise, He is married to the backslider. Do not become discouraged in prayer, and do not become weary in well doing - you will reap if you do not lose heart. Even if you sow in tears, you will doubtless come again rejoicing, bringing the harvest of your children with you!

Praying and believing with you for breakthrough.

Breaking Strongholds in Your Grandchildren - Born or Future

Grandchildren! What a blessing, and at the moment I only have one. But having five children, I'm quite sure that number will soon grow. Now, most of us don't have the privilege of raising our grandchildren with the same intimacy and closeness that we had with our children. Distance tends to diminish the time we can spend. My only grandson lives thousands of miles away from me in British Columbia, Canada.

But thank GOD for the power of prayer. Thank GOD that I can pray over my grandchild and you can pray over your grandchildren every day with instant access to the Throne Room of Glory and immediate connection with the GOD Who is their Father!

We are also blessed in this generation with incredible means of very close interaction. We Facetime with our grandson and what a joy it is to know that he recognizes our faces and voices. Distance no longer needs to be a diminishing factor in our closeness. Facetime, Facebook, email are tools for grandparents!

Valerie and I are determined to stay in each of our children's lives and our grandchildren's lives to be an example of steadfast love, a sense of security in their lives, and an example of faithful devotion to Almighty GOD and His Word.

I encourage you to do everything possible to keep speaking into your grandchildren's lives no matter their ages. Send them Christian books, Christian videos, Christian music; be a voice of Faith in their life, encourage them. They need to hear from you, they need to know you and your story.

"Only take care, and keep your soul diligently, lest you forget the things that your eyes have seen, and lest they depart from your heart all the days of your life. Make them known to your children and your children's children. **Deuteronomy 4:9**

"Children's children are the crown of old men", the Bible says in Psalm 17:6, and Paul reminded Timothy that his grandmother Lois was a woman of faith that started his GODly line. As you pray and fast today for your grandchildren, remember the scripture says that "a good man leaves an inheritance to his children's children." Don't over spiritualize this verse, it really is talking about money, seeking the blessing of GOD so that you leave significant surprises in your will for your grandchildren.

But don't leave the spiritual out of it either, we need to establish a Faith Legacy for our grandchildren. We need to daily uphold them before the Throne of Grace, that GOD would keep them in the hour of temptation, grant them a spirit of humility and repentance, and that their heart and mind and soul will be filled with the power of the Spirit and the Word of GOD.

We have the power as grandparents, as men and women of faith, to tear down strongholds in our grandchildren's lives in the Name of Jesus. We have the authority as Spirit-filled believers to claim the blessing of GOD for the generation to come. As you pray today for your grandchildren by name, begin to see them by faith, worshiping, prophesying, evangelizing, witnessing and living for Jesus! Fight for your grandchildren on your knees and watch GOD work wonders!

Praying and believing with you for breakthrough.

DAY 5 of 21-Day Breakthrough Fast
Breaking Financial Stronholds

It is day five of our 21 Day Fast for Breakthrough in every area of our lives! Stay strong in faith, spend time in the Presence of the LORD and extra time reading His Word and applying it to your life. Make sure to spend that time you would normally take preparing your food and eating, and various entertainments you're putting aside for these 21 days, alone with GOD.

Today we focus on Breakthrough in Finances! Let me encourage you with the simple truth that if you're GOD's child, you are subject to a Kingdom that is far above the recessionary, depressionary, inflationary forces of the world's broken/faulty/tax-laden economy! We are to pray daily "Thy Kingdom come, Thy Will be done on earth just as it is in Heaven." In Heaven, there is no lack, poverty or recession. There is so much prosperity in Heaven that instead of using asphalt for pavement, the Architect of eternal Glory lines His streets with gold!

But here on earth we do have our challenges, don't we? If you went to a doctor for a physical problem, he would ask for symptoms, and then begin to eliminate various causes until arriving at diagnosis, in the search toward the right steps to a cure. If we are in financial trouble, we can use the same process.

It's as simple as this. Am I working hard and am I working smart? The Bible says if I refuse to work, I should not be allowed to eat. Next, am I tithing? If I'm not paying GOD what is His, the top 10% of all my income, I am warned in the scripture that whatever my 100% is, it is actually under a curse. Also, have I been walking in wisdom? If you don't have sales resistance, have bought everything every credit card company has allowed you to, and you find yourself over your head- that's not GOD's fault.

So, what should we do? First of all, understand that GOD is a loving GOD of mercy, grace and forgiveness, to those who are humble and repentant! If we have financially failed our families and our future, we can fall on our faces and ask GOD for the mercy He has promised. Then ask for wisdom, start tithing, and then work as hard as you can to get out of debt *yesterday*! If you will begin today to be faithful, you will see a gracious GOD perform miracles of debt cancellation, helping you in ways you never dreamed possible, proving to you that the wealth of the wicked is laid up for the just.

GOD will do what only He can do, as we do what we must. I am not suggesting any of this is easy or automatic. Working hard actually means WORK! But living a debt-free life is more than worth any sacrifice necessary. Sell what you have to, downsize, live with one car if possible, and as I always say, in these turbulent times, quite seriously… "Pay GOD's Tithe, get out of debt, forgive and love everybody, plant a garden and buy a gun!"

I believe you can sincerely pray and ask GOD for creativity, energy, ideas, productivity, ingenuity and the spirit of an inventor! There are products, ideas and services that are yet to be created, so why not become their creator? After all, you're in touch with the Creator of the universe every day!

Our world is filled with stories and testimonies of believers who have had fabulously fantastic, financial breakthroughs, as they've begun to put GOD's Word into application in their lives. I am believing with you, and please believe with me, that you and I both will be the next testimonies!

Praying and believing with you for breakthrough.

Breaking Health Strongholds

What is better than healing? What is much better than a miraculous touch from Heaven when you're sick? There is something better, and that is walking in Divine Health, living with energy, sleeping well and having little or no pain in your body! Not getting sick is better than being healed of disease!

Living healthy should be our target, not stumbling from prayer-line to prayer-line, looking for the next great healing evangelist to lay his or her hands on us. Now, I believe in Divine Healing, I practice it and I've experienced the miraculous touch of GOD in my own life and body and I have been healed. I do lay hands on the sick and I do see them recover in the power of the Name of Jesus!

However, please know that GOD has placed much of the responsibility for physical health and well-being in our hands. If we are carrying 100 pounds of excess weight around our bodies we should not be surprised if our joints are screaming. If we are smoking several boxes of cancer sticks daily we shouldn't wonder why we are having trouble breathing. If we are carrying bitterness, anger and resentment in our minds and spirits, it is only reasonable to expect that those issues will get in our tissues and definitely show as symptoms in our physical bodies.

I have found in more than 30 years of personal and public ministry that the quickest way to access the power of Heaven to heal your body is to walk in absolute forgiveness, obey everything the Holy Spirit asks of you and then ask in faith, believing for the healing mercy of Christ's atoning work on Calvary to touch your body. GOD is still in the business of performing miracles! Healing is the children's bread! There is nothing impossible for GOD! There is no cancer, no leukemia, no arthritis, no circulatory, cardiac or respiratory problems, or any other kind of genetic or environmental-based ailment that lies beyond GOD's ability. He does wonders to prove He still has the power to forgive sins.

When GOD does not heal… when a loved one dies, please stay at least a million miles away from the Pharisees who judge, condemn and sanctimoniously declare that "someone didn't have enough faith." Neither you nor they are GOD, and some things we will not understand until eternity. Healing is GOD's business, and when He does not heal, it is NOT my business to determine why and then pronounce blame.

But until then, start living right, thinking and speaking right, start eating right, start moving and exercising, fuel your mind and spirit with the Living Word of GOD, because faith comes by hearing and hearing by the Word. If you need someone to pray in faith with you, we have a family of prayer warriors here who will agree with you by faith! Just e-mail me at mylesholmes@reviveusa.net

As you are fasting, expect renewed energy as your body detoxifies and cleanses from the junk food and excessive sugars. By the end of these 21 days, you may very well decide that NOTHING tastes as good as skinny/healthy feels!

Praying, fasting and believing with you for breakthrough.

Day 7 of 21 Day Breakthrough Fast

Breaking Strongholds in Mental/Emotional Health

Bless your heart and head! Today we focus on emotional and mental health, bringing them both into balance, by fixing and centering our lives on the Word of GOD.

In Luke 10: 27 Jesus confirms what we know instinctively. The human experience and existence is not only physical. It is not only emotional. It is not only mental, and it is not only spiritual. You are a compilation, a combination, an amalgamation of all aspects of human existence. Man became a living soul, we're told in Gen. 2:7

However, to ignore the spiritual/eternal aspect of your life is the most dangerous decision a human being can make. And, to ignore any of the other three aspects, physical, emotional or mental will eventually introduce you to frustration and limitations. But let me emphasize this again. The spiritual/ eternal aspect of your life is without question the paramount, preeminent, first priority of your life.

That being said, the physical aspects of your life will determine your energy level, strength, stamina, ability to concentrate, learn and memorize. The daily choices we make in diet, activity, rest, and so on help to determine the length of life and the energy we have to serve GOD and people. But look at how we're tied together as a human being. It is virtually impossible to separate the emotional state from the mental state from the physical state from the spiritual state. What you feel is prompted by what you think about, what you believe and by what you know. And what you think can be influenced by how you feel.

For the purpose of this focus, let's briefly consider the emotional state as related to the mental state. Just imagine with me, a scale of normal human response to stimuli, one extreme represented by the number 1 and the other by the number 10.

Let's think of the number 1 representing someone who is totally ruled by emotions, feelings, is moody and sensitive and is always reacting without thought. Now on the other extreme imagine a number 10 representing a person who is always purely intellectual, reacts out of mentally calculated reason, logic, cool and careful thought, perhaps best represented by Spock on Star Trek.

Now, consider how you normally relate to your world. What is your default emotional state? I am sure no one is a complete 1, or the other extreme a total 10, but where are you normally... a 4, 5, 6, 7? Do you tend to relate to the world more emotionally or more intellectually?

Now, here's where it gets interesting. Imagine yourself very tired, exhausted, worn out... where are you on the scale now? What about when you're hungry? How about when you've been hurt? What about when you're in a crowd? Or when you're all alone? Or when you are afraid? How do you react when you are feeling close to GOD? What about when you haven't been in the Word and prayer?

Of course, it is so important to realize that we are unique individuals, who act and react differently to varied stimuli. Where do you think the Apostle Peter would be on the scale? What about Paul? Some are more naturally intellectual, others more emotional. But health and wholeness, spiritual depth and maturity requires balance.

Let's think of some words to describe someone who is EMOTIONALLY unbalanced. We might describe them as fearful, jealous, sensitive, bitter, selfish, angry or moody. How will we describe someone who is MENTALLY unbalanced? We might say they're confused, distracted, unfocused, cold, calculating, detached, uncaring, unfeeling.

Now, we're beginning to see why emotional and mental balance is so critical in the life of a believer. So we must guard against any factors that lead to a lack of balance. Things like bitterness and unforgiveness. A lack of faith and a deficit of love and being double minded, the scripture says, all lead to a life of mind and heart that is out of balance.

So the question today is what must you know (mental) and believe (heart, soul, spirit, emotion) about GOD in order to live in a balanced state of heart and head? Here are a few starters...

1) GOD is Love and His Will is good for me. Romans 8:28
2) GOD is all-powerful and all knowing. Jeremiah 32:19, 27
3) GOD is my Father. Matthew 6:9
4) GOD hears my prayers. Matthew 6:6
5) GOD speaks to those who will listen. John 10:27

Meditate on these five truths for a few moments. Do you believe this?

And finally, what must you know and believe about yourself in order to live in a balanced state?

- I know I'm made in GOD's image and full of His Spirit. Genesis 1:26, 1 John 2:27
- I know I can do all things through Christ. Philippians 4:13
- I know I am forgiven, cleansed and under no condemnation. 1 John 1:9, Romans 8:1
- I know GOD has a perfect plan for my life. Jeremiah 29:11, Philippians 3:20, 21
- I know I can make daily choices to be an overcomer and more than a conqueror. Romans 8:37

You may want to make these statements a daily verbal affirmation for a while, until you believe them so completely that they become a part of your mental and emotional makeup, and then the truth will transform your personality into a permanent state of healthy balance.

Praying and fasting with you for breakthrough in every area of your life.

DAY 8 of 21-Day Breakthrough Fast

Breaking Strongholds of Pride/Rebellion/Stubborness

(WARNING-this teaching is not for spiritual babes, it could ROCK your spiritual world)

As we journey further in this fast, continue to earnestly and fervently pray for CHANGE, lasting permanent change in your life... your spiritual growth, your mental and emotional state and your PERSONALITY.

I am continually amazed by the number of Christians who have bought the lie that personality is inborn, static and permanently unchangeable. If that were true, the Gospel is a lie! It is not the truth. The TRUTH is, personalities, tendencies and default ways of acting and reacting can be changed by the power of the Word and the Spirit.

Which brings us to today's focus. As you fast and pray, ask the Holy Spirit to reveal to you any corner of your heart or mind where you harbor pride, rebellion or stubbornness. Fasting that does not confront sin in our lives is a worthless exercise in human futility. Fasting that opens the spirit to repentance is the doorway to miraculous transformation!

How do we evaluate pride, rebellion and stubbornness and why is this so important? Well, pride leading to rebellion is the original sin and makes us most like the father of all deception, the enemy of our souls. It is so important because pride goes before a fall, and will eventually strip our lives of anointing, fruitfulness and the sweet Presence of the Holy Spirit. The answer to pride, rebellion and stubbornness is asking the Holy Spirit to give you a heart of humility.

Humility and brokenness will welcome the healing power of the Holy Spirit to make us vessels fit for His use.

GOD resists the proud… (those who cannot be taught, cannot be corrected, cannot be instructed, those who know better than anyone else) GOD holds them off. But He gives grace to the humble. I want grace. I want to be truly humble… not humble like some people I know who are so proud of their humility they will let you know it. They have kind of missed the point, haven't they?

The truth is, humble people do not think less of themselves than others do, they just don't think of themselves at all. They're too busy thinking of blessing, helping, honoring and sharing their blessings with others.

As we fast, we are humbling our bodies, and our minds, we are surrendering our fleshly desires to a higher calling. Please join me in asking the Holy Spirit to root out even the smallest seed of pride, rebellion and stubbornness. The Bible says rebellion to authority is the same as the sin of witchcraft. Same root and same results. That's serious business!

I must have teachers and mentors in my life; I must have people in my life that can correct me, lead me and direct me. And so must you. That's why church involvement and submission to a strong, GOD-honoring, Word-teaching, Spirit-anointed, people-loving Pastor are critical to your spiritual development. If you think you've grown beyond that, you may need to fast for more than 21 days.

Humble yourself before the LORD, become accountable to spiritual leadership and whether you've served the LORD for 2 years or 5 decades, you will begin to develop new levels of spiritual maturity and miraculous blessing in your life. Remember that we only have authority as we are under authority. As we continue to walk in submission and surrender to the Holy Spirit, having a teachable attitude with a hunger to grow in humility, you will notice GOD opening doors of ministry that you've only dreamed about thus far.

Walking in a life of humility in no way should suggest a fearful, wimpy believer, scared of their own shadow! No, the righteous are as bold as a lion! We have not been given a spirit of fear but of power and of love and a sound mind. Let me help you with this simple thought. Proud people are self-confident, self-righteous and self- centered. Humble, spiritual believers are GOD-confident, righteous by the Blood of Christ and GOD and others-centered.

Fasting and praying with you for breakthrough in every area of your life.

Breaking the Stronghold of Prayerlessness

Most surveys report that the average Christian spends only three or four minutes a day in prayer with the average minister or pastor spending only a few more minutes a day alone with GOD! This would explain why many of our churches and ministries are so very average when it comes to impact and productivity. On this ninth day of our fast, let's determine to become above-average prayers, excellent intercessors and powerful prayer warriors!

If you are involved in any sort of public ministry, let me warn you that I do not believe GOD honors exclusively public prayers to the benefit of your personal life. In other words, if the *only* praying you do is heard by others, seen by others, enjoyed by others, you will have no authority or power with GOD. You absolutely must develop a personal daily *alone* time with GOD!

However the converse is also true. If you cannot pray in public, if you cannot open your mouth to worship GOD and seek His Face in front of other people you must repent of shyness and false humility. Then realize that to be worried about what people think of you would be to suggest that you're praying to them instead of to GOD! We must stop comparing ourselves to others and how we measure up to their style of emphatic, prophetic, loud or demonstrative praying. If that's not you, don't worry about it, but pray and pray much you must.

You can learn to pray, and like the disciples you can ask the Lord Jesus, "Teach me to pray", and He will. Make a commitment right here and now, not just for these 21 days, but for the rest of my life, I will keep a daily audience with my King. I will report in for my marching orders!

Now, let's look at what prayer really is and what it means.

PRAYER IS NOT....

...convincing God, it is not the believer's gripe/complaint session, it is not changing God's mind or twisting God's arm.

PRAYER IS THE...

- Engaging of faith in the revealed will of GOD...
- Entrance to the Throne Room of mercy and grace...
- Environment to which GOD restricts His workings...
- Enforcement of GOD's rule upon a rebellious world...
- Enjoyment of GOD's tangible Presence...
- Enduing of our lives with power...
- Encouragement of mind and spirit with truth...
- Enriching of personality with GOD's peace and purity...
- Encounter of human weakness with Divine strength...
- Encampment of stubborn faith upon the promises of GOD...
- Enterprise above all others for growing, effective Christians.

Let's bury, once and for all, the old lie that some are "gifted" or "called" to be intercessors, and others are not. Show me in the Word of GOD where there is a "gift" of prayer. Show me in the Bible where you can find the "office" of the pray-er. You can't find it. All GOD's children are called, expected, anointed and appointed to pray.

We all have the wonderful privilege of praying GOD's will on earth, just as it is in Heaven. Our churches are as weak as our prayer lives are pathetic. Our ministries are as strong as our intercession is prophetic. You have not, because you ask not!

Ask In Faith!

Ask with anticipation!

Many make a study as to why prayer is not answered. Books have been written on that theme. I have even preached a few messages on that topic. But I would much rather be an expert on why GOD does answer prayer!

GOD answers faith-filled prayers. GOD answers persistent prayers. GOD answers fervent prayer. GOD answers the prayers of righteous people. GOD answers prayers of agreement. Find a group of people, or even just one, and agree together in prayer. Keep a prayer journal. Record your miracles. Those who expect nothing in prayer are never disappointed.

Expectation!

Faith is a prerequisite, a Bible-condition for answered prayer. If you want to receive any response from Heaven, you must believe that GOD is, and that He is a rewarder of those who earnestly and consistently seek Him. So let your faith arise. Go ahead, let GOD's promises get your hopes up. GOD rewards expectation. So pray, pray without ceasing, pray in faith and GOD will answer.

Strong in Prayer!

We are as strong spiritually as we are strong in prayer. We are as effective spiritually as we are effective in prayer. We are as fruitful in our lives as we are dedicated to prayer. We are as productive for Christ as we are committed to prayer.

Prayer is work, a battle, a warfare. Prayer is peace-producing, a joy and delight. Prayer is a struggle, a labor and requires commitment. Prayer releases power, strength and comfort.

Don't be confused; prayer is all of the above and must consist of all the above. Those who find prayer to be only a battle and a fight are not engaging the victory won by faith. Others who only experience prayer as a joy and delight, have forgotten that we are at war with the forces of hell. Fight on! Pray on! Laugh through tears and celebrate the victory that overcomes the world, even our FAITH!

Fasting and praying with you for breakthrough.

DAY 10 of 21-Day Breakthrough Fast

Breaking the Stronghold of Fear

Far too many of God's people are controlled, manipulated and weakened by fear. Fear of the future. Fear of their past returning to haunt them. Fear of financial trouble. Fear of people. Fear of FEAR. Fear is intimidating, exhausting and debilitating. It is a thief that steals energy, joy, motivation and vision.

But it need not be so. The Bible proclaims that GOD has not given us a spirit of fear but of power, love and a sound mind. Notice one important fact that the Bible clearly shows us. Fear is a spirit!

Of course, we are not talking about exercising reasonable caution. Boldly walking across thin ice because you "do not have fear" is exhibiting a lack of wisdom, not an absence of fear. The technical term for this attitude is actually "stupidity"!

No, the fear of the LORD is the beginning of wisdom, so we must always walk in wisdom, founded, grounded and bounded by the parameters of the Word of GOD. The 'spirit of fear' the Bible speaks about is what must be broken by the Truth of GOD's Word. Recognizing fear as a spirit, an un-holy-evil-hellish power is the first key to total victory, because only then do we realize we need a spiritual solution! And a spiritual solution always starts with the Blood of Jesus, the power of the empty tomb, the Living Word of GOD, and the abiding presence of the Holy Spirit.

Spirits can be fed generously or purposely starved to death. What are you feeding your mind, your eyes and ears? What are you always THINKING about, dwelling/meditating on? Spirits can also be destroyed by the anointing! That is

Bible. Spending time in the Presence of GOD diminishes every other distraction. Spirits can be silenced by the voice of praise. That is Bible, too! When you feel afraid... WORSHIP! PRAISE! SING! DANCE! It works EVERY time!! Spirits of fear cannot stomach being within earshot of any praise of Almighty GOD! (Compare Ps. 8:2 & Matt:21:16 PRAISE SILENCES THE ENEMY)

Believers must understand that fear and doubt activate, motivate and authorize satan to work in their life and experience. Faith and trust invite, empower and release GOD's Presence and Purpose in your life. We must determine daily and moment by moment WHO our attitude, actions and speech will activate and motivate in our lives. Will I speak that which invokes a spirit of fear, or will I speak what releases the Power of the Word of GOD and the Blessing of Heaven in my experience? You will repeatedly have what you repeatedly say. You will consistently experience what you constantly verbalize.

Faith comes by hearing and hearing by the Word of GOD. The best antidote to a life of fear is time in His Presence and in His Word. May I put it this simply? GOD is afraid of nothing! If you are His child, He is your ABBA. There should be no room in your life for a debilitating-weakening-worrying-energy-sapping spirit of fear.

Martin Luther was experiencing yet another grievous trial in his life and became quite afraid, fearful and depressed. Seeing his sad state, his wife went upstairs, changed into her mourning clothes, wearing black from head to toe, came back downstairs, walking very sadly through their home. When he finally noticed her, Marty asked, "I'm so sorry. Who has died? I hadn't heard." She responded with mock surprise, "Oh my, I assumed from the way you're acting, GOD had died! That we no longer could pray or ask for His help or count on His promises, His Presence, or His Word. Surely, Martin, GOD has died hasn't He?" Martin got the message, smiled, gave his sweet, dramatic wife a kiss, got up and shook off the lies of the enemy, and was launched on to greater victories.

So, as you fast today, you might want to get somewhere and SHOUT (into a pillow if you have to) "GOD is alive! Jesus lives! His Word is true! I believe His promises! I will NOT fear, because nothing, absolutely nothing, can ever-ever-ever separate me from the Love of GOD which is in Christ Jesus, and His Perfect Love casts out all fear!" Shout OUT the DOUBT & the POUT! Shout it OUT in Jesus' Name. (you can stop shouting now…or better yet, keep on shouting and bring your shout to church this Sunday!)

Praying, fasting and believing with you for total breakthrough.

Breaking Strongolds of Anger

Stay strong in faith today as you fast, pray and seek the LORD. Today's focus is asking GOD for a breakthrough in the area of any anger issues you must confront. Since this is such a weighty topic, let me start with a bit of humor.

A husband once said to his wife, "I'm always so angry and mad at you and yet you never fight back. How on earth do you control your anger?" She answered, "I simply go clean the toilet bowl." "How does that help?", he wondered. "Oh, I just use your toothbrush!" (By the way, that remedy for anger is certainly NOT recommended.)

I have had a lifelong interest in this subject for two reasons. First, I have noticed that angry, bitter people often die younger than happier people and have more long-term health problems. Medical research has now proven that prolonged periods of anger actually suppresses the immune system. Second, is even more serious, and that is the sad reality that Christians who are consistently angry and bitter tend to have children who don't serve GOD.

The good news is, there is hope for hotheads and there is an antidote to anger. It starts with obeying the Word of GOD. James tells us we should be swift to hear, slow to speak, slow to wrath, because the wrath of men does not produce the righteousness of GOD. Remember your mother telling you to count to ten before speaking? Slow to speak. She got that wisdom from the Bible.

Proverbs 16:32 says "He who is slow to anger is better than the mighty, and he who rules his spirit better than he who takes a city."

This is really a discussion of spiritual, mental and emotional maturity. We are not overly concerned when a three-year-old throws a temper tantrum when he doesn't get his own way. It's a much more serious issue when a 53-year-old uses emotional outbursts of anger to control and manipulate.

You know the old cliché is true, an angry person is seldom reasonable and a reasonable person is seldom angry, because the emptier the pot, the quicker it boils.

Some claim that they cannot control their anger. We know by experience this is simply not true. Have you ever seen a person change their attitude the moment they have to answer the phone? We can turn off the rage and turn on the sweetness in a matter of seconds. This proves that anger is a manipulative tool that is used consciously for personal benefit.

Anger can be a real detriment to our Christian witness as well. A police officer was following a very angry driver who was honking his horn at everybody, waving his fist in the air, yelling out the window at the 'stupid jerks' in his way. The officer pulled him over, asked for license and registration, looked him up and down and finally said, "OK, have a good day." The angry driver said "Officer, why did you pull me over, what did I do wrong?" "Oh, it's simple, when I saw the bumper stickers on your car that said, 'Honk if you love Jesus' and "My boss is a Jewish carpenter' I naturally assumed this car was stolen!"

Here are seven things you need to know about unrighteous anger.

1. When anger is rewarded it is repeated.
2. When anger is suppressed, it is dangerous to your health.
3. Anger that is used to manipulate somebody you are to be submitted to, is rebellion, which the Bible equates with witchcraft.
4. Anger that is used to control those in submission to you, is violence, which the Bible says GOD hates.
5. Recognize that anger is only a symptom, the cure lies at the root. Anger sprouts from pride, foolishness, immaturity, self-centeredness, cruelty and malice.
6. Don't get furious, get curious. What is your anger telling you about you? How much of this anger is related to your lust for control? How

much of this anger is related to your rights? Or your impatience? Or your stubbornness? Ask yourself, 'Whose name (reputation, glory) is on the line?'

7. Stop internalizing your problems. Yield your rights, do good to those who despitefully use you. Walk in forgiveness and patience. Grow the Fruit of the Spirit found in Galatians 5. Understand that every one of these Fruit are the direct antithesis of anger... 'Love, joy, peace, long-suffering, kindness, goodness, faithfulness, gentleness and self-control.'

As you fast today and ask GOD to break the stronghold of anger in your life, or in the life of someone you love, I can prophesy three huge benefits derived from living in peace with a calm spirit. First, when we no longer explode, we will not have to clean up our messes anymore. Second, allowing the LORD to help us maintain a calm spirit will enable us to regain our family's respect. And finally, being in control of our emotions means our Christian witness will be more believable and therefore, much more effective.

Time is too short, the hour is too late for us to continue to battle the results of our angry outbursts instead of fighting the enemy of our families and our souls! Lay down your rights right now, declaring, "I don't need to be first, I don't need to be right, and I don't need to be noticed. I just need to be like Jesus." That's what the Gospel and the Power of the Holy Spirit is all about, transforming ME into HIS image! And it certainly does not hurt to count to 10, or 20 or 30 before we act, react or speak out of emotion. Then, there will be a much greater chance that what we share will bring the King glory and not shame.

There is a time and a place for righteous anger, the kind where we are angry without sin, as the Bible says. Almost as dangerous as the man who is always angry, is the man who is never angry. Stand for truth, for Christ, for liberty and defend the weak, but be clothed with meekness, which is velvet-covered steel! Meekness is power under control. Be filled with His Spirit!

Praying, fasting and believing with you for total breakthrough.

Breaking the Stronghold of Resistance to Change

If you are one of the handful of people in our world who never struggle with change, keep reading, because I will provide you with some tools to help the vast majority of the world and the Kingdom who often struggle with adapting to new things and new ideas. This should not be the case, as the Bible makes it clear in 2 Cor. 5:17 that if we belong to Christ, we have become a new person, the old life is gone and the new life has begun.

The child of GOD is to be a change agent. A conversion catalyst. An engineer of revolution. A minister of reconciliation. An architect of alteration. An instrument of transformation. We are GOD's agents of change in this world.

When you forgive someone, the world has changed. When you love, the universe is a little different. When you act kindly towards a stranger, the world is not the same. When you express love to your spouse or family, the world has just changed. When you open your hand to share with no expectation of return, when you open your mouth to share the good news, when you lift someone's burden, cause a worried face to smile, you have touched the universe and nothing will ever be the same again! Change your world. If not here, where? If not now, when? If not you, who?

The Gospel of Jesus Christ is a ministry of change, and the Kingdom of GOD is an environment of transformation. The Church of Jesus Christ is a place where change is expected, encouraged, and celebrated. I am not what I used to be, and neither are you. We have changed. I am not what I'm going to be and neither are you. We are changing, we are growing, deepening, maturing and developing.

But we also understand that there is more often than not a natural resistance to change. We also see that those who need to change the most often are the most resistant to change!

However, the world gives bold witness to the fact that those who have learned they have the power to *choose* change, become the Champions at Life! They have learned if they want different results they must do something, and perhaps many things, differently.

Let's pause for a brief theological lesson starting with a question. If you are redeemed by the Blood of Christ, when did you stop changing, the moment you were born again? Certainly not. In fact, that is the moment we *start* changing!

So, why do we resist change? It is because it threatens our sense of security and our comfort level. We resist change out of a reverence for a particular tradition that we have misinterpreted and mislabeled as 'Holy'. We resist change because it may mean we lose control, power and position. We resist change because of human pride. We tend to only really love change if it's MY idea. Finally, we resist change because it affects my identity.

The stark choice could not be clearer. You will either be a Champion of Change or a Child of Chance! In order to embrace the change that is required to grow you might want to look at this Change Challenge.

- CHECK for the positive in every experience.
- CHART a different course of reacting.
- CHOOSE an attitude of faith.
- CHANNEL your negative response into positive action.
- CHAIN yourself to GOD's unfaltering Word.

We must not resist change, we must welcome it, but only with this protection and guard at the gateway to change. Almighty GOD, and His Word never change. Jesus is the same yesterday, today and forever. His Word is forever settled in Heaven!

The most successful and joyful people in our world all share a common but vital trait- the ability to adapt. They can quickly adjust in new situations and circumstances not only accepting change, but grasping it as an opportunity to expand and grow.

I am determined not to resist change, but to be an agent of transformation in a world that so desperately needs the power of the Gospel of CHANGE!!

Fasting, praying & believing with you for total breakthrough.

DAY 13 of 21-Day Breakthrough Fast

Breaking the Stronghold of the Inability to Keep My Mouth Shut

Our words are incredibly important! Speech has the power to build, create, bless and encourage. The same tongue can unleash hurt, pain, discouragement and destruction. James 3 tells us that your mouth can get you into a pile of trouble!

The Bible says that in a multitude of words, sin is not lacking. Proverbs 18:21 says that death and life are in the power of the tongue. Words can start wars, create enemies and deeply wound. But words can also heal and bless, bringing comfort, peace and understanding. The right words can literally change a life.

James 1:26 says that, "If anyone among you thinks he is religious and does not bridle his tongue but deceives his own heart, this one's religion is useless."

Jesus cried out (in another one of those moments when he wasn't being very meek and mild, and non-offensive), "Brood of vipers! How can you, being evil, speak good things? For out of the abundance of the heart the mouth speaks. A good man out of the good treasure of his heart brings forth good things and an evil man out of the evil treasure brings forth evil things. But I say to you that for every idle word men may speak, they will give account of it in the Day of Judgment. For by your words you will be justified, and by your words you will be condemned." Matt. 12:34-37

Now, that is pretty strong stuff and a stern warning to those who speak without thinking- whatever is in their head and their heart has to spill out. Proverbs 18:2 describes this person saying, "Fools have no interest in under-standing; they only want to air their own opinions."

Think on this, GOD never speaks an empty or idle word. Neither should we. If you have nothing to say, then don't say it. Talk about others the way you want them to talk about you.

Realize you are becoming whatever you think about and talk about consistently. Your words create the environment you live in. Your words create the world you inhabit. Your words create your spiritual environment. Do your words welcome the Holy Spirit or grieve, quench and resist Him?

You are never more like the devil than when you are speaking gossip, accusation, slander, discouragement and destructive words. Satan is the accuser of the brethren.

You are never more like your Heavenly Father than when you speak life, blessing, hope, faith, grace and help; words that create, instead of destroy.

Your words create an atmosphere where GOD can create. GOD spoke and there was! GOD said, "Let there be." And it was! GOD spoke the cosmos, the universe, light, space and time into existence by the spoken word and He made us in His own image with the power to create by our words. You say it and it is! You say I'm afraid, and you fear! You say, I can't and you can't! You say I won't and you don't! You say I'm clumsy and stupid and pronounce all kinds of foolish curses on your life and wonder why you're not doing better!

How about changing your vocabulary to include statements such as "I am greatly blessed, highly favored and deeply loved! I am a child of the Living GOD, and I have the Mind of Christ. I am blessed coming in and blessed going out. I'm washed by the Blood of the Lamb and I am the devil's worst nightmare! I'm filled with the Holy Spirit and I am strong and anointed to do exploits because I know my GOD. I can do all things through Christ. Greater is He that is in me than he that in this world. No weapon formed against me shall prosper!"

Your words are so powerful because they declare what you are in agreement with. Jesus told us to "Have faith in GOD." For assuredly I say to you whoever SAYS to this mountain, be removed and be cast into the sea and does not doubt in his heart, but believes those things he SAYS will be done, he will have whatever he SAYS."

Determine today to delete some stinkin' from your thinkin' and erase all the whiny-weak words from your vocabulary. Impossible, defeat, retreat, failure, etc. will no longer be options. Practice SAYing, and believing these kind of words more often …blessed, favor, repentance, restoration, prosperity, victory, harvest, health, FAITH!

The Bible tells us one day that a voice will be heard in heaven saying, "Now salvation and strength and the Kingdom of our GOD and the power of His Christ have come, for the accuser of our brethren who accused them before our GOD day and night has been cast down. And they overcame him by the BLOOD of the Lamb and by the WORD of their testimony." GET this! Jesus DID it, and we have to SAY it!!

So, maybe better than keeping our mouth shut, is actually opening our mouths and start declaring good things and great things, decreeing GOD things!

Scientists and psychiatrists are only now discovering the incredible power and connection between your spoken word and your conscious belief system. Of course, GOD knew this all along because He created us human beings. But now the astounding advances in science, brain-imagery and medical understanding are showing that we only really accept as fact what we have HEARD ourselves SPEAKING in our own voice. We only truly believe that which we have verbalized for ourselves. There could be a clue here as to why FAITH and our WORDS are so inextricably entwined in the Scripture! Believe it. Speak it. Act on it.

If we truly want our speech to change, we must ask the Holy Spirit to change our hearts. A heart of love, grace, patience and understanding will spill over with those kinds of healing words!

Fasting, praying and believing with you for total breakthrough.

DAY 14 of 21-Day Breakthrough Fast

Breaking the Stronghold of the Tolerance of Sin In My Own Life

Keep your hearts and spirits open to the voice of GOD as you fast and pray today. Just a little more than a week left in this season of miracles and breakthroughs!

JESUS - "You might want to get that LOG out of your own eye, before trying to help your friend with the speck in theirs!"

Today we turn to a very important focus, and that is letting the Holy Spirit search our hearts and cleanse us from anything grieving, quenching or resisting His Presence and Power in our lives. Our tendency to judge others, criticize and point our fingers while ignoring our own sin does not please GOD. He loves us enough to ask us to change in this area.

Of course, there is the tendency in the Kingdom to swing from one extreme to the other. Some are so legalistic and religious that they believe they can perfect themselves and others around them if they only try a little bit harder. They tend to be cruel, judgmental and self-righteous, and absolutely no fun to hang out with, let alone go to church with!

On the other extreme is licentiousness. That's a wonderful, old King James word that means, 'anything goes, I've got a 'license to sin', a 'get-out-o'-jail-free card' because I'm under grace.' The Bible makes it plain that neither of these work in theory, in practice or in building righteousness. Ephesians tells that we are saved by faith, and that faith is the gift of GOD. It's ALL grace, or we'd all be boasting about the good work we've done.

But the balance between legalism and cheap grace is found in allowing the Holy Spirit's convicting voice to lead us in ways that please the LORD. No condemnation, no self-righteousness, but a desire to live in a way that brings GOD glory!

So the question is, am I open to a gentle rebuke, correction, direction and instruction by the Spirit? Do I allow GOD to speak to me about my attitudes, my thought life, my speech, the way I spend my time? Do I do I invite GOD to help me make decisions about the movies I watch, the television I enjoy? Can I watch scenes of excessive violence and sexuality, with no sense of GODly conviction? Do I really believe the Lord Jeusus laughs at the things my flesh finds 'funny"? Do I soothe my conscience by insisting that I am adult, mature and can handle this?

I am more than convinced that the demonic debauchery spewing out of Hollywood would cease almost immediately if every sincere Christian would ask the Lord for discipline in this one area. The economic toll on Hollywood would be devastating.

Today as you fast and pray, ask the LORD to reveal to you any way that you can grow more and more like Him. Then repeat the prayer of John the Baptist, 'He must increase, I must decrease.' Understand the Scripture that declares we have become partakers of the Divine Nature, and glory by glory, we are being transformed into His Image.

No condemnation, just life and hope. No guilt, no fear, but a limitless universe, full of GOD's Love and Grace.

Timothy Keller, in his foreword to the excellent book BONHOEFFER by Eric Metaxas, puts it like this. "There is a brilliant balance of the Gospel that Luther so persistently expounded, 'We are saved by faith alone, but not by faith which is alone.' That is, we are saved, not by anything we do, but by grace. Yet if we have truly understood and believed the Gospel, it will change what we do and how we live."

Live in Grace, for yourself and for others, and grow in Grace, which means more and more and day by day reflecting the Glory of Who Christ is on this earth!

Fasting, praying and believing with you total breakthrough.

Breaking the Stronghold of Addiction to Food

A season of fasting and prayer is a great time to ask the LORD for deliverance from our addiction to food. Addiction to food? Isn't food a vital necessity, isn't an appetite a GOD-given gift?

Of course, a proper appetite is natural, good and necessary for health. In fact, a lack of appetite is a sign of disease and diminishing health. However, the truth is, many of us eat far too much, and far too much of the wrong food. When you crave sugar, sweets and salt and have trained your body to be satisfied and comforted by the wrong kind of food, you have developed an addiction that you need deliverance from.

The Bible says we must glorify GOD in our bodies. (1Cor. 6:20) We must understand that our body is a Temple, the only earthly home we will ever have, and our enjoyment of this life is greatly determined by our health. Your ability to earn income is affected by your health. Your ability to play with your kids and grandkids, to maintain mental alertness, are all dependent upon your health. The ability to sleep soundly at night, enjoy intimacies with your spouse, all are greatly determined by your health! It is difficult to think of any area of our life that does not suffer when we do not take responsibility towards our health.

Remember what George Burns said… "If I'd known I was going live this long, I would've taken much better care of myself!"

Lifestyle choices we make every single day will help you determine not only the length of life we live, but its quality as well. Choices like what we eat, and how much, how we think, how we exercise, can all actually help determine when and how we die. It may sound severe, but you must admit you have something to say about whether you die peacefully in your sleep at 105, or drop dead from a heart attack while climbing the stairs to your bedroom at 55.

So much of our health is a matter of personal discipline, NOT genetics or environment. The book of James in the Bible ends with the encouragement to pray for the sick in the Name of the LORD and the prayer of faith will heal our bodies. What is interesting is that earlier in this letter James reminds us that faith without works is dead, ineffectual and worthless.

In other words, stop praying for your health unless you are willing to begin to make the changes required to support a healthy body. Would it make sense to ask GOD for a new heart and circulatory system when He knows we have no intention of giving up that bucket of fried chicken and gallon of ice cream that our poorly trained appetite craves and is addicted to?

The point is, we must take responsibility for our health. Perhaps the strongest Biblical warning regarding our health-disciplines comes from the same book of James in 4:17, "It is sin to know what you ought to do and then not do it." Do you know that you should lose weight, eat better, exercise more, and change your attitude? Then if you don't do it, you are in sin. Disobedience. Denial. You call it what you want, GOD calls it sin. The Bible is painfully direct, but purposefully honest. There is hope for better health as we ask for GOD's help with self-control and discipline.

Weight management is all about the proper discipline of eating and moving, moving and eating, eating and moving. Eat less, move more. Eat better, burn more fuel! Amazingly, try it, you can experiment, and you will find it to be true that man CAN live without candy, cakes, chocolate bars, donuts, potato chips, french fries and cookies. Not only live, but live longer, healthier and happier.

If you're on a total fast, and you have been for these past 15 days, let me shout HALLELUJAH with you as you rejoice in the fact that you have been delivered from any addiction to salt and sugar! And the good news is, as you've broken these habits for 21 days, you can live this way permanently!

You probably have not lost much weight on this fast, as your body has a way of storing fat during these non-intake days. But as you go back to eating sensibly, fruit, vegetables and lean protein, staying away from fats, sugars and excessive salt, you'll begin to see the massive changes in your health!

Never again look to food for the COMFORT that we can only find in His Presence!

Ask the Holy Spirit for His guidance, discipline and assistance in growing all the fruit of the Spirit in your life which includes self- control. Every addiction, every bondage, every fleshly appetite that does not honor GOD is broken by the anointing. And by the way, "Nothing tastes as good as skinny feels!"

Fasting, praying and believing with you for total breakthrough.

DAY 16 of 21-Day Breakthrough Fast

Breaking the Stronghold of Lack of Passion for the Lost

Set yourself apart with GOD today and ask yourself a very serious, soul-stirring question… "Do I even care a little bit that thousands of people all around me are rushing to a CHRISTLESS eternity, headlong to hell with no hope of rescue?"

Today we are asking the LORD to somehow awaken our hearts and reignite our passion for the lost. When is the last time we spent a sleepless night weeping and travailing in prayer over the unsaved condition of loved ones and family and neighbors? When was the last time we witnessed to someone outside the grace of the Gospel? When is the last time you heard a strong message on the reality of hell, the wrath of GOD and the consequences of living and dying in spiritual rebellion?

One of the very first signs of revival is a renewed passion for the lost! If we do not care for the souls of mankind that Christ shed His Blood for, then we need to question our own relationship with GOD.

We can so easily get caught up in our own pursuits, seeking blessing, working hard, even laboring diligently in the Kingdom, that we forget why we are here. The Kingdom is not a cruise ship, the Church is not an amusement center for your personal enjoyment and comfort, the Church is to be a Coast Guard rescue vessel out on the stormy seas rescuing the perishing! The sailors on a Coast Guard ship have never complained to the captain, "Hey, don't rock the boat!" No, their whole mission is to go out on the storm to save another soul!

When we constantly complain about the music, the choice of songs, the volume in our church services while at the same time never inviting a single soul to join us and hear the gospel, something is wrong with our passion! When we criticize the Body, can't find anything good to say about the leadership of our church, we have lost our vision. And when we lose our vision, people perish!

It always amazes me that grandparents would give their lives, take a bullet or jump in front of a moving train to save their grandchild's life, but they absolutely refuse to compromise on any kind of change in church tradition that might reach the younger generation! It would be funny, if it were not so sickly sad, sinful and tragic.

People are going to hell without Jesus, and it's way past time we start caring about that!

Not long ago I was with a group of Christian leaders and I was shocked by one statement. He was a young, hip, trendy, bold-confrontational, 'don't care what you think', in-your-face type of preacher. None of that bothered me, we were all young once... but what he said grieved my spirit.

In a discussion regarding how we preachers handle rejection, he blurted out, "I just tell people, 'You don't want my Jesus, then just go to hell, I don't care!' " There was a weak chuckle in the room, someone changed the subject, and we moved on.

I don't know him, or his name and I want to be as fair as possible to this young man- give him every possible benefit of the doubt. Any preacher of the gospel, must have a GOD-confidence, that he is called, and not be swayed by man's opinion. At times we shake the dust off our feet and say, "You haven't rejected, me you have rejected GOD.' I certainly hope that's what this young preacher meant. But his cold, callous demeanor did not suggest that his heart was broken over the lost. I remember that Jesus, looking over Jerusalem, WEPT TEARS OF SORROW at their rebellion, unbelief, lack of repentance, and all that meant for the city's future. (Luke 19:41) The cocky-casual-careless attitude of this preacher toward souls made me weep for him!

Please let your heart be broken over souls, pray for revival and a glorious harvest! Pray that your church and your pastor receive fresh Fire-from-Heaven that will ignite every pew-warmer with a holy determination to get out in the highways and byways and by all means win some! Pray that your altars are filled this Sunday morning with souls being saved, backsliders reclaimed, and cold hearts set ablaze! This is why the Holy Spirit came, to make us WITNESSES!

For all the preachers, teachers, prophets and evangelists reading this, let me share with you my paraphrase of what Spurgeon shared with his ministry students. (Don't let the humorous intent blind you to the deeper message behind it.)

"My future preachers, be sure to preach often on Heaven! And when you do, be certain that your face shines with the glory reflected from its golden streets, make sure that your smile is lit up with the radiance of the City with no night, be certain that your facial expression expresses pure Mercy and Grace, while your whole countenance beams with Celestial Light! Now, ministers, also be sure that you preach often on hell, and then, well, your NORMAL face will do!"

Praying, fasting and believing with you for total breakthrough.

DAY 17 of 21-Day Breakthrough Fast

Lack of Submission to Spiritual Authority

Prepare yourself, some toes may be stepped on here, because this problem is a world-wide, trans-border, multi-generation EPIDEMIC in the church! Kids catch this disease from their parents and grandparents! I am in no way suggesting that this is a new problem, in fact you can find it throughout the Bible.

The New Testament declares that even Jesus Christ could not do many mighty works in his hometown because there was no recognition of His Anointing, there was no faith in Who He was or what He brought. Ananias and Sapphira died in the Presence of GOD because they lied to the Holy Spirit and to the spiritual authority they were speaking to, Peter. Read it carefully in Acts 5; they thought they were lying to men only, that was the grievous error!

However, although we can find many more instances in Scripture and history of people so full of spiritual pride and rebellion that they totally lost out with GOD, I must suggest that our modern age makes us much more susceptible to this temptation. It is very difficult for anyone in this generation or the past couple to grasp how very different our world is from the last several thousand years of human history. If there is one thing that marks our time, is that people are in love with their own opinion and demand that they answer to no one because "My highest authority is me!"

Now, I am in no way promoting group-think or herd mentality or any loss of personal liberty and individuality. Thank GOD that we are free from religious and the need to please any man! However, that personal freedom has also brought with it a temptation to believe that I am not to be in submission spiritually, that I can set my own agenda with GOD, and I will answer to no one. And that my friends, is dangerous both for time and eternity.

This attitude is often demonstrated by those who declare. "I am very spiritual, I just don't believe in organized religion!" What a ridiculous statement. We appreciate absolutely everything else in our lives being organized, but not religion.

Try going to an unorganized restaurant. No menu, no prices, haphazard service - wouldn't work would it? What if your employer decided it would be an unorganized workplace? Maybe you will get your paycheck, maybe not. Perhaps you have a job next week, perhaps not. Would you be interested in watching an unorganized sporting event? No rules, no referee, no actual object of the game, no winners or losers?

I could continue with all sorts of silly examples but you get my point. The vast majority of people who say 'I'm not into organized religion', really mean 'I don't want to have to answer to anyone, and I don't want anything expected of me, I can do this on my own, thank you very much.'

Now, anyone who knows me, knows my constant motto that 'relationships matter more than rules and people matter more than policies.' However, the Lord has established spiritual authority in our lives. If we cannot be committed and submitted then we are living in rebellion.

Can your pastor speak loving correction to you? Can he or she give you loving direction when you are a bit off track? Do you have a teachable spirit, or a know-it -all attitude that is insulted and offended if anyone dares to question your decisions or beliefs?

Many Christians believe that they can continue with slander, criticism, gossip, defiance and rebellion against their spiritual authority and have the Holy Spirit be okay with it. They have ZERO respect for the gift, calling or anointing that is in front of them, and then they wonder why GOD is not answering their prayers!

The Bible has a warning for those who will cause their pastors who watch out for their souls, to give an account of them with grief instead of joy! Believe it or not, it all hinges on how we *obey* our spiritual authorities. (Hebrews 13:17)

Now, if that bothers you, that would be because you have a problem with the WORD, not me!

But let me assure you that the LORD does NOT expect you to submit yourself to anyone who is compromising Biblically, doctrinally, morally, financially or acts like a tyrannical dictator. May GOD deliver His church from angry preachers who have little mercy, less grace and even less love. Pastors must care for, watch out for, LOVE the Body and the lost, not for personal gain but because they are eager to serve GOD..."Not acting like a lord, but leading by good example." 1 Peter 5:2,3 Keep looking, find a spiritual leader like that, and grow under his or her anointing.

A Pastor/shepherd must LEAD the sheep into new places, new fields to graze in, new visions and fresh anointings.

A Pastor/shepherd must FEED the sheep with nourishing, nurturing life-giving teaching from the Word of GOD.

A Pastor/shepherd must GUARD the flock from the wolves of deception, false doctrine and from the wolves sent to sow discord and dissension.

It's a big job that cannot be done without the Presence, the Power and the Anointing of the Holy Spirit. Pray for your pastor/preacher, he or she is certainly human, but they're also divinely called and equipped, appointed and anointed to be a blessing in your life. YOU decide whether or not to receive that blessing!

If you ever expect to walk in authority, please understand you will get there by walking UNDER authority, NOW.

There are many today who suggest that they don't need a pastor or a local church. They are perfectly satisfied to worship GOD on Sunday morning under a tree, or at Starbucks, or climbing a mountain or on a golf course. These are not pagans, these are people who want you to believe they are sincere followers of Christ, but have no interest or time or affection for the Church of Jesus Christ, the Body of our LORD on the earth which the Messiah bled and died for.

I would suggest that this is a not-so-subtle rebellion against GOD's plan that we live in submission to a spiritual authority that is watching out for our souls. If this is you, repent, and begin to obey the Word. Then you will not forsake the assembling of ourselves together with the family of GOD and so much more, as you see the return of the LORD drawing near.

Today as you pray, ask the LORD Jesus for a humble spirit, a quiet attitude and a teachable heart. If you need to humble yourself and ask forgiveness from a spiritual authority, go ahead. If they are a man or woman of GOD, they have ALREADY forgiven you, but you do this to protect your own heart! You will be absolutely amazed and wonderfully blessed at the anointings and ministries that GOD will open up for you as you serve where you are right now.

If you are faithful in little, GOD will make you ruler over much, and besides, little is much when GOD is in it!

Fasting, praying and believing with you for total breakthrough.

DAY 18 of 21-Day Breakthrough Fast

Breaking Strongolds Over our Nation

Today we are fasting, praying and believing for a mighty revival to sweep across America once again! It is time for another GREAT AWAKENING! How dare any of us say we are too far gone! How dare any of us say that GOD will not hear our prayers! How dare any of us pretend our GOD is so small that He cannot do something so great as to shake this nation one last time with a mighty move of His Spirit!

Hear me clearly! The answer for America will not be found in our court systems. The answer for this nation will not be found in our educational institutions. The hope for the USA is not found in electing the right politicians!

You certainly must vote. A Christian who will not vote is personally responsible for the moral bankruptcy of our nation. Soldiers bled and died to win you this privilege, so use it. Vote wisely and prayerfully, not blindly for a party, but carefully vote for righteousness.

We may do well however, to remember the warning of Marcus Tullius Cicero of Rome who wisely noted that, "Philosophers view all religions as equally bad. The common man views all religions as equally good. Politicians view all religions as equally useful."

No, the hope for this nation does not lie in courts, media, universities or political parties. The future of this nation lies in the churches and pulpits of this great land! As John Stott declared, "We should not ask 'What is wrong with the world'? That diagnosis has already been given. We should ask rather, what's happened to the salt and the light?"

The last great move of GOD in this nation will start with a work of the Spirit in the Church, sparking a revival of righteousness, holiness and separation from the lusts of the world, matched by a burning passion to tell the Truth, to fight evil and to win the lost at any cost to the Love and Mercy of Jesus Christ. For far too long the church in America has been more concerned with popularity than purity, more interested in acceptance than anointing, more concerned with income than iniquity and more in love with marketing than ministry! It's time for the church once again to be a prophetic voice to this generation.

Pastor Martin Niemoller in Nazi Germany was one of the few preachers who withstood Hitler to his face. "You will not tell me when to preach, or where to preach, or what to preach, or how to preach."

His boldness resulted in intensive interrogations. For months the Gestapo came to every church service, sat in the front row with green leather trench coats on, writing down every word of this preacher. Eventually he was arrested in the middle of the night and thrown in jail with the drunks and prostitutes and vomit and filth.

In the morning the resident chaplain came by and was shocked to recognize Pastor Niemoller. He asked, "Dear pastor, what on earth are you doing in here?" The pastor responded to the chaplain, "With all that is happening in our nation my friend, the real question is, 'Why are you not in here?' "

Until we are willing to pay any price, lose any friend, spend many a sleepless night in prayer, give to our last penny, endure any mocking and scorn, until then we will WAIT for revival.

It is way past time to answer the call of the old hymn, "Stand up stand up for Jesus, ye soldiers of the Cross, lift high the Royal standard it must not suffer loss, from victory onto victory, His Army shall He lead, till every foe is vanquished and Christ is LORD indeed!"

Is revival possible? The answer to that query is another question. Is there anything too hard for GOD?

A better question may be, is revival promised? And the answer is yes, the Word of GOD declares, in the last days the Spirit will be poured out upon all flesh! The last time I checked, flesh lived in America, Canada and every nation of this earth.

You and I have to decide whether we'll be a hesitator of revival, an imitator of past revivals, a spectator of revival (sitting back watching & hoping to see something) or will I be an INSTIGATOR of revival, a RESUSCITATOR of a mighty move of GOD?

You want a revival? Do as Gypsy Smith recommended. Take a piece of chalk, draw a circle around yourself on the floor, and say to GOD, "Send revival inside this circle and I will not let You go until You do.'

I am standing strong in faith with you in these last four days of fasting for a supernatural move of the Spirit in your life and mine that will spark a Jesus-lovin', devil-hatin', sin-erasin', red-hot, Blood-bought REVIVAL in our circles, and *that* can only spread!

Down through the decades, through many generations, prayer warriors and saints have fasted, wept, and travailed in prayer for GOD to turn this nation back to the faith of our founding fathers, back to the Word and the principles of righteous living. Let's determine that we will be the answer to those prayers, realizing we have come to the Kingdom for such a time as this!

Fasting, praying and believing with you for total breakthrough.

DAY 19 of 21-Day Breakthrough Fast

Breakinging Strongholds Over the World & Israel

Is anybody singing that great old chorus anymore? "LORD, lay this world upon my heart, and love this world through me, and may I ever do my part, to win this world to Thee."

Thank GOD for every missionary, every missions effort, every cross-cultural- international apostle and evangelist who are reaching multitudes for Christ around the world. What about your heart, does it beat heavy with a passion to see a harvest from every tribe, tongue, people and nation? Do your prayer times include fervent intercession for South Africa, Brazil, Moldova, North Korea, Saudi Arabia, Russia, etc.?

Thank GOD that we understand individual and personal salvation, but our hearts simply must expand to grasp a vision big enough to take in the whole world that Jesus died for.

- For God so loved the WORLD.
- Behold the Lamb of GOD which takes away the sins of the WORLD.
- The earth is the LORD's, the WORLD and all that is in it.
- The WORLD is Mine and all its fullness.

These and many other scriptures are evidence that GOD wants us to en-large our inheritance beyond, "GOD bless me, my wife, two kids, us four & no more."

If you are longing for the return of Christ, then DO what He said. Get this Gospel to the ends of the earth and then He will return! Pray, give, and when possible GO to another nation and spend some time with your brothers and sisters in the Faith.

I cannot begin to tell you what GOD has implanted in my heart as I have ministered in China, Israel, Haiti, Trinidad, Jamaica and other nations outside of the US and Canada. I know that I always receive much more than I give during these seasons of ministry.

While you are praying for the world, remember Israel, remember Jerusalem. Our Jewish family is surrounded by nations and ideologies of pure evil and hatred, consumed with the desire spawned in hell to destroy every last evidence of GOD's promise to Abraham. We simply must stand with Israel. We must pray, and we must publicly and loudly support Israel's right to defend herself. And again, when possible, GO to Israel! What a blessed and rich experience it is to walk on some of the same stones that Jesus walked on in Jerusalem, to visit the tomb that is EMPTY, and to worship the Lamb near Golgotha!

As you pray for our world today, remember our persecuted brothers and sisters. Remember their chains and pray for their liberty.

I am grateful for and supportive of many wonderful ministries that exist to encourage the Body of Christ to remember our persecuted family around the world. I join the letter-writing campaigns to dictators in other nations and I email and write our incompetent or uninformed senators and congressmen here in the USA. But I am greatly bothered by a consistent pattern I have observed.

There are wonderful calls to prayer and support, and appeals for money and involvement, concern and commitment but what is far too often missing is an appeal to pray for deliverance and freedom! When there is a well-known name and face that can be identified with a family, then this rule is broken. However, there seems to be a regular system of denial when it comes to seeking GOD for deliverance from captivity, torture, persecution, prison or death.

I encourage you to monitor this with me. Just last week I received a prayer bulletin from one of these wonderful ministries. Included was a 10-point plan of intercession. Things like peace, grace, strength, love, the ability to forgive the persecutors, and the protection for this ministry's teams as they travel internationally. All of that is incredibly important of course, necessary and very Biblical.

What was missing from the letter, brochure and these 10 points, however, was any suggestion of praying for their release, freedom and deliverance. Not a mention! That is shocking and unfortunately too often, very consistent with too many of these ministries.

I am more than aware of all the individuals suffering for Christ who get messages back to the west with no suggestion of a prayer for deliverance or freedom. That speaks of their discipleship and commitment to Christ, it says nothing about our responsibility as to how we should pray for them.

David prayed in Psalm 7 "Oh, LORD my GOD, in You I put my trust, save me from all those who persecute me and deliver me, lest they tear me like a lion, rending me in pieces, while there is none to deliver."

Paul escaped from death at Damascus by being let go over a wall at night in a basket. He was delivered from his persecutors because it was not his time.

An angel delivered Peter from prison miraculously as he was being prayed for by the church.

GOD sent an earthquake to set Paul and Silas free from their shackles and prison cell in Philippi.

These and other miracles of deliverance helped to establish the Church of Jesus Christ.

I don't pretend to know everything GOD is doing, but I will declare with loudest voice and with great authority that we must begin praying once again for freedom, deliverance, liberty from captivity, torture and persecution, and for protection of the Body of Christ around the world. To do less is selfish and faithless. I can assure you that if it was your brother or your sister, if it was your flesh and blood, you would be praying for something more than just that they find peace and grace in their hour of trial.

It is once again time for earthquakes, angels, baskets, miracles, signs and wonders!

Pray big, bold prayers for this world that Jesus died for! Pray as He told us to, 'Thy Kingdom come, Thy will be done, on earth, just as it is in Heaven.' Pray in the Spirit for the nations. And realize that often as you are praying in tongues, you are praying in a native earthly language, the perfect Mind, Will and Plan of GOD for that people.

JESUS died for Buddhists, Muslims, pagans and Hindus. He shed His Blood for atheists and animists, witches and satan-worshippers. His Glory is found in redeeming His lost lambs out of every tribe, tongue, people and nation. It should be our greatest joy to pray in that harvest, and work for its reaping.

Nothing, absolutely nothing is impossible for GOD, so we can pray, expect and believe for a mighty, earthshaking Revival in these last days. That's what I live for!

Join me in the quest for a renewed passion, a willing endurance and a holy persistence that will not be satisfied with anything less than the greatest Harvest the King has ever received!

Praying, fasting and believing with you for total breakthrough.

Breaking Strongholds Over our Church

Just two days left in our 21 days of fasting for breakthrough, and these next two days we are going to focus our praying on our church.

Now, when I say our church, I really mean HIS church, not simply the one that I have the particular privilege of pastoring right now. This includes your church, which is also HIS church, because the true church doesn't belong to any of us but to Christ alone.

So, today as you pray for breakthrough in the church, I want to talk you about the force that releases favor and the power that produces Pentecost. There is an energy, that when released can touch families, churches, nations and kingdoms.

If the church, the Body and Bride of our LORD Jesus Christ would once and for all understand and utilize this force, the kingdoms of the world would much sooner become the kingdoms of our LORD and of His Christ! The church will become a true force to be reckoned with in every city. The Body of Christ would become the visible and literal manifestation of the Life and Power of the Resurrected Christ, slaying every dragon of doubt, smashing the gates of hell and shining the Gospel light of love and signs and wonders into every dark corner of our world!

The power and force I am speaking of is the power of UNITY!!

This power is terribly dangerous in the wrong hands, but OH, so precious in the hearts of the holy! Scoffers and mockers, the complainers and the critics, the enemies of this energy will deny its potential, and go on living their lives weak, weary, wimpy and ineffective. Others will pick up the torch of UNITY, see its incredible resources, and declare by the grace of GOD, by the help of the Holy Spirit, "I stand on the promises of GOD and I choose today and every day to have this power in my life, this force in my favor, yes I will, I will walk in UNITY. Unity with my brothers and sisters. Unity with the family of faith. Unity with the brotherhood of believers."

Jesus prayed in John 17:21-23, "That they all may be one, as You, Father, art in me, and I in You; that they also may be one in us, that the world may believe that You sent Me. And the glory which You gave Me I have given them, that they may be one just as We are one. I in them, and You in Me, that they may be made perfect in one, and that the world may know that You sent Me, and have loved them as You have loved Me."

- Romans 16:17 I urge you brothers, note those who cause divisions and offenses contrary to the doctrine which have learned, and avoid them.
- Titus 3:10-11 Reject a divisive man after the first and second admonition, knowing that such a person is warped and sinning, being self-condemned.
- Proverbs 6 These six things the Lord hates, yes seven are an abomination to him (last of the seven) … one who sows discord among his brothers.

I will choose every day to walk in unity, because I don't have an option, a choice or any discussion in the matter. I must put away strife, anger, selfishness and sin. I must forgive my brother and sister and never harbor bitterness. I must choose to walk in love and harmony because I am not going to miss the glorious fruit of unity.

When somebody tries to speak against your brother or sister, you say, "Hey, wait a minute, that's my brother!" When someone comes against your pastor, say, "Hey wait a minute, that's my pastor!" When someone speaks against your church, say, "Hold on, that's the church of the LORD Jesus Christ and you can't talk about my family like that!"

You see, in the family of God, we belong to each other, we matter to each other, we take care of each other, we value one another. Because there really is no red or yellow black or white, rich or poor, big or small... we are all precious in His sight! We are one in Christ Jesus and as we strive for this unity, doing our best to be at peace with all men, we recognize this unity is not based on compromise but it is based on truth. This unity is not based on overlooking sin but forgiving sin.

When we walk in unity, we are reflecting the image of the Triune God, the Holy Trinity. The perfect union of Father, Son and Holy Spirit, perfect intimacy and closeness, perfect agreement and harmony, perfect holiness and righteousness, perfect power and authority and perfect oneness. If we desire His blessing, presence and glory, we will live, walk, speak, dream and minister in UNITY! The devil trembles at the very thought of a church like that.

Remember, JESUS did not promise to build a Congress, a Senate, a Court system, a Parliament, a Knesset, a nation or a democracy. The Bible warns us that these days of everything being shaken that can be shaken would come. Christ *did* promise, "I will build MY church, and the gates of hell will not prevail against it." Seems to me a very safe place to be is somewhere inside what the Son of God is building!

It would be wise to make certain that you are part of His church, and that this weekend, you gather with His People to worship Him and hear His Word. See you in church, Church!

Fasting, praying & believing with you for total breakthrough!

Breaking Strongholds, Releasing Revival and Harvest!

This is the last day of our 21 Day Breakthrough Fast. For those who have joined me on a complete fast, I invite you to join me tomorrow morning in splitting a pound of bacon. You can have half!

More seriously, be very careful in resuming eating. Resume very slowly, and why not stay off of the excessive sugar, salt and fat? For good! But once in a while, treat yourself to a crispy piece of the good stuff. Now, back to business.

As I stated yesterday, when I say our church, I really mean HIS church, not simply the one that I have the great joy of pastoring. This includes your church, which is also HIS church, because the true church doesn't belong to any of us but to Christ alone.

At the end of these 21 days, it is time to prepare for revival and the harvest by doing what only you can, so that GOD will do what only He can!

<u>What is Revival?</u>

- It is not hype!
- It is not a religious side-show!
- It is not a spiritual carnival of MAN-infestations!
- It is not a display of emotionalism, although emotions will be involved.
- It is not an angry, legalistic, judgmental, critical spirit.
- And, revival is not optional!

<u>Revival is!</u>

- A return to a passionate love of Jesus Christ!
- A return to the preeminence of preaching!
- A return to the power of the Word!
- A return to a pursuit of holiness!
- A return to the place of prayer!
- A return to a JOY-filled enthusiasm for Kingdom Life!

This world, your church, your city, your family needs revival because…

- the harassed need a hiding place,
- the hungry need a home,
- the hurting need a helper,
- the heartbroken need a healer,
- the hell-bound need a hope and His Name is Jesus!

Claim the Word of GOD, a promise for Revival, let the Truth ignite Hope in your heart and Faith in your spirit.

- Isaiah 57:15 "For thus says the High and Lofty One Who inhabits eternity, Whose Name is Holy: I dwell in the high and holy place, with him who has a contrite and humble spirit, to *revive* the spirit of the humble, and to *revive* the heart of the contrite ones."
- Habakkuk 3:2 "O LORD, I have heard Your speech and was afraid; O LORD, *revive* your work in the midst of years!"
- Psalm 85:6 "Will You not *revive* us again, that Your people may rejoice in You?"
- Isaiah 64:1 "O, that You would rend the Heavens! That You would come down! That the mountains might shake at Your Presence!"
- 2 Chronicles 7:14 "If my people, who are called by My Name, will humble themselves and pray and seek My Face, and turn from their

wicked ways, then I will hear from heaven, and will forgive their sin and heal their land."

Satisfaction and nostalgia are two of the greatest enemies of the harvest and of revival. An obsession with today and yesterday, can prevent God showing up tomorrow! Let go! Let GOD!

Those addicted to comfort, security and tradition have locked themselves in the safe harbor of yesterday and never risk the venture of new Oceans of Possibilities! If you are not ready, willing and excited for GOD to do something New/Bold/Fresh/Creative, you have not been reading the Word, and you, my friend, are in the way!

"It's my way or the highway!" … is the talk of a highwayman! (definition… thief/robber, brigand)

The love of tradition/rules/policy has prevented more great moves of God then false doctrine! Keep in mind that Religious- Rules- Keepers killed Christ! But He got up! Creative minds do not discard or destroy the old, trusted truth, but attractively message it for new generation.

Charles Finney gave us a great recipe for revival that is so needed today. "Revival comes from Heaven when heroic souls enter the conflict determined to win or die- and if need be, to win and die! 'The Kingdom of Heaven suffers violence and the violent take it by force.' A revival is both as natural and as supernatural as a farmer planting corn in the ground and expecting a harvest of corn! Both man and GOD are involved in the process!"

GOD is willing. Will you show up?

Will you continue to pray as you never prayed before? Will you continue to repent in humility like you never have before? Will you continue to give, as you've never given before? Will you continue to invite, invest, promote, plant seeds, witness as you never have before? Will you continue to love the LORD supremely and love the lost deeply and stop worrying about anything else? Will you continue to daily determine to make Jesus Christ the absolute Sovereign LORD of your life? Would you be willing to make more room for GOD?

If your answer is yes, or even an honest, "I want to want to", then this fast has been a success in your life! Today is not an end, it is the beginning of a new relationship with GOD. What an ADVENTURE we are on!

I would love to hear from you as to what these 21 days have meant in your life and your spiritual growth. I would also be honored if you continue to connect with this ministry where ever you can find us on Facebook, Twitter, Linked-In, WordPress, etc. I send out an encouraging word several times a day.

I live to be a Faith-Coach Motivator to GOD's people and spark revival wherever I can. May GOD absolutely astound you with His overwhelming love, mercy, blessings and grace!

I will continue to pray for you, that every single aspect of your life experiences total breakthrough!

About the Author

Pastor Myles Holmes is an ordained minister with the Assemblies of God. He has preached the gospel of Jesus Christ in Asia, the Caribbean, South America and throughout the US and Canada. He and his wife Valerie enjoyed many years of daily television ministry which was broadcast around the world on TCT, TBN, DayStar, and other networks.

They are active in evangelistic ministry, sharing the Word of the LORD wherever GOD opens doors. However, Myles Holmes's greatest passion is the local church. He has been the Lead Pastor in two churches in Canada and now has the privilege of serving GOD's people at REVIVE in Collinsville, Illinois, 12 miles east of St. Louis.

Myles and Valerie Holmes are the parents of five children and one grandchild. Their ministry is one of biblical balance, strong encouragement and a bold, prophetic word wrapped in love and grace.

You may contact them by email at mylesholmes@reviveusa.net or on Facebook at *Myles Holmes Ministries*.

Myles and Valerie Holmes are available for ministry in campmeetings, conferences, retreats and church settings.

Made in the USA
Middletown, DE
16 January 2019